Names

How To Name
Your Start-Up Venture

DAN GUDEMA

Names: How To Name Your Start-Up Venture
Copyright © 2016 by Dan Gudema

All rights reserved. No part of this book may be reproduced or transmitted in any form or by any means without written permission from the author.

ISBN-10: 1505339057

ISBN-13: 978-1505339055

DEDICATION

This book is dedicated to Jeromi Stewart, who listened to me and renamed his product on the spot. That event led me to believe that I actually had some talent in naming and renaming products, services and businesses. I am also dedicating this book to all the tech start-ups who are trying to create jobs and ultimately wealth.

DAN GUDEMA

CONTENTS

INTRODUCTION 5
MEMORABILITY 25
FAMILIARITY 33
PERSONALITY 41
HUMOR 49
MAGNETISM 59
NAMES ARE MARKETING 67
BUSINESS NAME VS. PRODUCT NAME VS. DOMAIN NAME .. 75
UNCONSCIOUSLY NAMING 87
THE NAME SHORTENING GAME 95
NAME EXAMPLES 101
HOW TO NOT NAME YOUR COMPANY 117
A FEW FINAL WORDS 129
THANKS TO THESE STARTUPS 131
QUOTED PEOPLE 133
YOUR READING LIST 135
ABOUT THE AUTHOR 137

ACKNOWLEDGMENTS

Thank you to Tom, Donna, Norman, Madeline, Michelle, Ron, Jonathan, Rachel, Linda, Victor, Max, Jeanie, Michael, Brian, Justin, Noah, Shira, Devorah, Shana, Jacob, Craig, The Anthonys, The Davids, Gigi and Olivia for having to listen to me talk about writing books. I want to acknowledge Gary Kahn, Amanda Anthony, John Kemp, Marc Cherenson, Rachel Lebensohn, Mike Lingle, Terry Aronson, Adam Kravitz, Marc Wigder, Brian Gibson, Mark Laymon and other people who give as much as they take.

The number 1 Question to answer in choosing a business name is do people remember it!

DAN GUDEMA

Introduction

It was July 2010. I was attending my first CEO Space meeting in Henderson, Nevada, in the hills outside Las Vegas. Jeromi Stewart happened to sit down next to me. Jeromi was a young hippy-like entrepreneur from Portland, Oregon.

The room was filled with several hundred people talking, laughing and standing around.

Jeromi was about to pitch his new kind of dental floss product to a couple hundred potential investors.

CEO Space runs this very special pitch event called SNAP. You run around with a silly hat on and pitch to groups of 5 to 10 potential accredited investors or partners at a time for up to 3 minutes a group.

Jeromi was on deck about to go and do his SNAP. I had just met him. Jeromi looked at me and described his floss sticks, spinning them around holding one end. There were 2 sticks on both sides and floss down the middle. I immediately recognized a pattern! That pattern was the shape of Num Chucks, a martial arts instrument that has been around for centuries.

And then I blurted it out. "Call them Gum Chucks!"

Jeromi gave me a confused look and said "You really think I should change the name?"

Jeromi had 30 seconds left before the pitch.

We stared at each other for a second in that chaotic room.

My tone got deeper and authoritative. I told him to "Just Do It!"

Jeromi had 10 seconds left before his pitch.

He had to make a quick decision whether or not to change his product name in his pitch!

He decided right then he would go for a name change.

The result was every time he spun the floss sticks around and announced the name, "Gum Chucks" the group of investors would laugh. He already knew he had a winning product with a great design. Now Jeromi knew he had a winning product name!

Over the next 6 months, Gum Chucks raised $1.5 million in startup capital from investors. The company became Oralwise, which has developed a series of innovative dental products for children and teens. The name change was the tipping point.

This book will give you insight into why certain names work for your product or service and why others do not.

I just want to make sure you understand that I am not a guru, nor an expert. The information in this book is just my opinion and intuition. I could be incorrect in my assumptions, but as you will see naming is all about intuition and there are no rules in the end, other than do customers or users adopt the name.

There is no exact recipe for success in coming up with a name for your start-up venture. Quite often the name of your venture and your product come to you in an instant. That's how it usually works for me! Your gut tells you this is the name!

So you would think, why do I need to read a book

about business, service and product names if these names come to us so readily?

We all can think of company and product names right now off the top of heads. The problem is you can end up generating a hundred names that don't make sense or don't feel right.

The answer is, even though you may be great at generating names like most people, you still need to know which ones make sense from a business and psychological perspective.

First we need to do a deep dive into why certain names work and what you are looking for!

My Basic Naming Theory

Coming up with a name for your product or business is not always easy. Names are intangible, opinion driven and innate. They either work or they don't work! What you love the next guy will hate.

If you look at some brand names over the past couple of years like Godaddy, Monster, Uber or Plenty of Fish, you would think, anything goes. However, there is a rhyme and a reason to why these name stick. I say stick, because that is what you are looking for in a name. Sticking means it stays in your brain for some reason and you can't get it out!

In the dating business which I work within, I came across the name "Oops I'm Single" for one of our dating business names. The name initially does not come off as fantastic in the online world of domains, because it has too many beats (4 syllables). It has too many letters and is too long according to domainers (12 letters). It has pretty much no value to domainers (people who horde and sell domains) or for search engine optimization (the business of getting found better on Google and other search engines). So you get the point, domainers are not always right about names!

Oops I'm Single has no value according to Sedo, the place you buy and sell domain names! Yet, when I had a beautiful logo made up and share it with people who have never heard of it before, I almost universally get one of several reactions.

One reaction I have received was "I have heard of this!"

No they haven't! I had just created it! So, let's call this **familiarity**.

Another reaction I get is laughter. Let's call this **personality** and in some cases **humor**.

Finally I often get an "I would try that", even though they don't know the actual value proposition or benefits of the product or service. Let's call this **magnetism**.

These are the qualities you want in a great name. These are the qualities in great digital brands like a Godaddy.

Creating A Great Brand The Old Fashion Way

Let's get into the ways brands, names for products and businesses have generally been created before the Internet boom.

The first way of creating a great brand is just letting it happen naturally. Often this is the town name or the name of the founders like Sears & Roebucks, New York Magazine or Macys or it could be the actual name of the physical product or service like Coca Cola.

There is nothing special about these names in the beginning other than they are often family or town names. The entrepreneur or you would be building that brand from the ground up. Eventually, years later you would have an old time brand with a culture and history to it that goes way back.

The old fashion way of using your family name sounds crazy in today's world of rapid business cycles. It is time consuming. It would literally take a lifetime the way they did it. This is how most familiar brands started and grew.

You may be competing with these brands with an archeological and historical history. We know many like Sears and Coke. They are strong. They have staying power. They will be around long after we are gone. That is great for them! But as you can see, if you don't have the luxury of waiting 50 to 150 years, you need to find a better answer, now!

If you are competing with some of these long held brands, you need to understand who they are and why they have built a fortress around these names in order to break through their brand walls.

Buying A Brand

The second way to get a strong brand name is to buy your way in and force the brand name to exist.

You come up with a sensible enough brand and then hit the public airwaves on TV, radio, print and Internet with massive ad campaigns to make people never forget the name. With unlimited funds, you could run ads night and day until your market gets it!

Marketers have done a great job in certain cases to convince you that a brand is what it is. It costs time and money to do this. Companies spend millions to essentially brainwash the public that the brand is synonymous with their product or service.

Marketers will try to convince you to associate a name the old fashion "Mad Man" way to make a brand. That is the story of many brands that we consider great brand names. A good example of this in the modern period is Match.com. My mentor mentioned to me recently that when he hears Match.com, he thinks Soccer Match. Maybe it's because he grew up in Scotland. That is what most people would have thought about Match.com before they undertook a great advertising campaign, which they continue to run today. It worked amazingly well.

The big downside to spending your way into creating a brand is you have to continue to train the public that you are who you are. That is why we see a Match.com ad every night on network TV.

There are several problems with buying your brand name. Eventually that brand name needs to become more flexible to change with the future. But once the public has set an idea in their brains about what that brand represents, that brand may not be able to flex and change. And once again change requires paying for the public to understand the new brand.

Canadian Tires Is More Than Tires

A great example of an historical brand evolving over time is "Canadian Tire". I am from New Jersey, so I had never heard of Canadian Tire. So to my surprise Canadian Tire is much more than tires. This is an institution in Canada which rivals Wal-Mart. Who would know this? Canadians! It has become a memorable name for them, but for much more than the name. They make long term associations with the name. Canadians think of their childhood and sometimes even their own mortality.

Great brand names go much further in getting loved and adored by their followers. The impact of a great brand is not just psychological, it is emotional and can be on the level of religion. This was proven by Martin Lindstrom, the author of Buyology, a book I recommend reading.

Lindstrom also developed a psychological concept of finding pieces of your brand that stick indefinitely in a customer's mind. He came up with the concept of Smash Your Brand. The idea came from the logo on a glass coca-cola bottle. Whenever a glass bottle of coke would smash on the ground, the bottle would break but the logo would remain intact because the glass under the logo was raised higher up.

Ultimately you want a brand that sticks to your subconscious.

What Martin Lindstrom recommends is a test for Internet sites. Cover up the website logo. Without your brand name will customers instantly recognize your brand. Smashing your brand means removing the brand words and seeing if customers can still recognize it.

Will your new brand name or existing brand name be embedded in the customer's brain from a visual or subconscious perspective? That's what you are trying to accomplish when creating your brand name. You want to be a subconscious icon that people keep in their heads and feel a personal connection with!

Unique Names Born With Panache

The third way to create a brand name from scratch is to discover and introduce a brand so unique and memorable that people will easily recognize it and never forget it! Yes, this means finding a brand today with every possible domain that exists out there already purchased!

But domain names do not matter as much as you think. You can do it if you are not focused on the domain name, but rather the brand name!

Your name has to stand out as something different yet be easy to understand.

Still the most importantly point is, can people remember the name?

A good example I ran into is a web development agency in Pittsburgh called "Branding Brand". Sounds kind of silly, right? Well, there is a message in their name. It is that they are the brand that brands others. And most important I never forgot their silly name!

Can a 5 year-old look at the brand and tell what you are doing? There is this old saying that you need to create a brand and company name where people get it right away. "We Deliver Paper" is a name that you get. They deliver paper. This a good and simple answer if you just want to be average. But it is better than a name that is completely unrelated! However, it is not that memorable and ultimately that could lead you to failure. The long term problem would be if you no longer delivered just paper or paper at all. It would be a problem and you would have to change the brand name.

I remember a pizza place in Sunny Isles Beach, Florida where I lived called "Hungries". At least that is what the sign said! The problem with the restaurant name and sign was nobody got it. All the cars passed their great sign position on A1A near the beach. I had never entered the door. Meanwhile nobody understood what it meant and that they had great pizza. They even tried to simplistically come up with a name which referred to eating. In their attempt, they missed everything we are going to discuss in this book. Just grabbing a random verb or misspelled name and not thinking carefully about the brand aspect can be the end of your business!

When I first came up with "Oops I'm Single", I asked a ton of people what they thought of my new dating site name. There were some amazing reactions. The name was exactly what we were looking for. It was unique enough to tell you it was about dating. It imbibed something different and unusual. There was a double entendre or double meaning in the name that could be taken in several ways. People remembered it and joked about the name whenever they saw me. They would say "Oops here comes Dan again" or "Oops I'm Divorced". They could love it or hate the name, but most important they never forgot it!

You will know the right name when you hear a name that makes sense to you. When people start asking you about it and they remember it weeks after you first told them! That's when you know you have found your name.

Names By Chance

I was at an event listening to Tom Monaghan, the founder of Dominos Pizza, speaking to a crowd. He was talking about why they were called Dominos. They had originally been called Dominic's Pizza in

Lansing Michigan. The owner of Dominic's sold Tom and his brother the business and moved to a new city. The brothers went as far as they could with that name delivering pizza. One day they got so successful they expanded to a second city. At that point, the original Dominic contacted them and told them that they could no longer use that name by law. They had to change their name. Eventually one of the pizza delivery guys arrived back from delivering pizza at the university. He complained that students keep getting the name Domnics wrong and were calling him the "Domino" guy. Once Tom heard that name, he jumped on it and grabbed it. So, keep your ears and eyes open. A name could be right in front of you, as we speak.

Can You Recognize Good And Bad Names?

Look around your world. The business names on the stores and restaurants in your neighborhood have certain meanings. They can be about pizza, sushi, vaping, dry-cleaning. Try to understand why they came up with that name and if you think it is appropriate. Come up with a better name for their business!

NAMES

Through-out this book we are placing exercises and writing space to help you figure out how to come up with a name. Just follow the exercises and it will start the process for you.

NAMES

What are your "key words" that need to be either in the name or referred to in the name?

_____
_____
_____
_____

Put together a list of the competitor names and see how they make a pattern that your name should fit.

_____
_____
_____
_____

When did you have that "Aha" moment (when you knew there was a product or service to create)? Write down this moment carefully and look over the words you used to describe it.

_____
_____
_____
_____

DAN GUDEMA

Business names can reach deep into our psyche and become part of everyday culture

DAN GUDEMA

Memorability

Are you looking to find a name for your next start-up? Well, you may have to come to right place. Am I going to come up with your tech start-up's name? No! You have to figure that out. I can, however, give you some unique tools to help you in your search and a few tech naming stories along the same. You should, after you read this book be a bit of an expert on names yourself!

When we were trying to come up with a name for our up-start speed dating event business in 2001, the founder told me that he had found a name. It was a name that was acceptable he felt, but not exceptional. We were determined to go into the speed dating business, and the name was available as a domain and as a trademark. We were not that excited about it, but succeeded in making the name work. We would become "Pre-Dating" or "Pre-Dating.com". It was not a bad name. It was an appropriate name from the perspective of our motto "Pre-Date before you date". However, we both knew deep down inside that our name was not that memorable.

We made the name succeed, but quite honestly for

many years to come people who attended our events could not remember which speed dating company they attended. The same was true of the two other top speed dating companies; 8Minutedating and Hurrydate to a lesser extent. The market was a bit of a commodity play, so people really did not understand our value proposition compared with competitors. Speed Daters could not tell the difference between the companies. We would get a call from customers who attended competitor's events and vice versa. You would think they could remember the name of the company they had attended! They could not differentiate our company names! It all started with our name. All of the speed dating companies had names, but no serious brands!

How Do You Find A Name That Is A Brand?

You start by finding a memorable name? Quite honestly, luck is a big factor. You can do it. It is not something you can expect to happen immediately, though it can happen in an instant. You need to at least commit to becoming a bit of an expert on creating names yourself, at least within your own industry. Being a history buff, studying religion, sports, trivia, being a member of World of Warcraft and being an avid reader all help.

Some people may say it is hard to find a name that is not taken, in terms of domain names. I disagree. I have less faith in domain names than I do in brand names. Brands don't have to be exact domain names. They can be slightly off in terms of domain or name as long as they are something people can remember.

One thing I tell people all the time (and I took this from David Tyreman, see the index of people I mention in the back of this book) is reach forward in your business model to what you ultimately produce for the customer. This means that you need to find a name that does not exactly state what you do today, but rather what you ultimately do tomorrow for the customer. Ultimate names are more memorable overall. For instance, my favorite name in the dating business is eHarmony, simply because that is ultimately what they produce.

Sometimes a memorable name has more to do with a weird name or jingle like Monster, Amazon, Pandora or Godaddy. Notice that these names pretty much focus in on living things, myths or places. Memorable names sometimes go off in a childish direction bringing your mind to embed it deep inside. These names have some psychic dust on them that sticks to you and they don't let go. We will be talking about them long after they are gone...

How to get started in finding a memorable name?

Start with thinking about your business and the ultimate goal of what you are trying to produce for people. If you are a financial services firm, you may be ultimately finding your customers peace and happiness. Use those words or similar words in your name!

Think of a list of the most memorable business names you can think of? Trust me, you will know them. Write them down below and read them over. What makes them stand out?

_____
_____
_____
_____

If you have come up with some potential names for your business write them down here. Circle the ones that you believe are memorable.

_____
_____
_____
_____
_____

Carry this book around and mention some of the names you are thinking of to people. You can even email them. Wait approximately a week or longer. See if they can remember the name you mentioned.

_____
_____
_____
_____

Your name will therefore seem like it is familiar to the buyer or client and therefore they will think they know it.

Familiarity

You ever get that deja-vu feeling? There is something about places, people and things that remind us of something else. We get this feeling we have already had this experience before. We think we know this person already. We feel this object in our hand is something we have already known before.

It's happens to all of us at some point in time!

Places we go, people we meet and things in the world all have similar traits.

You can recognize patterns, especially in people. As you get older you see the same things in people that you have already seen years before in previous people and relationships. They are different, but in some ways they are repeating themselves. The world is made up of repeating patterns.

You need to take advantage of these repeating patterns in our heads in order to find a name that people feel they already know.

It is not an easy task!

If you can accomplish finding something familiar in your name, you will have conquered one of the major problems with business and product names that do not connect with people. Your name will therefore seem like it is familiar to the buyer or client and therefore they will think they know it.

This is not some Jedi Mind Trick! It is a simple truism of life.

One pattern of one thing is similar to another.

Everything we look at reminds us of something else we know that is similar.

If you take this concept and apply the following process, it will make some sense to why certain names work.

For instance, let's say you wanted to come up with a name for your new tech company which makes a ***Time Management App***. You need to take a visual picture in your mind of an object that is going to remind you of your product.

NAMES

So, what is that object?

You could choose a thingy. For instance a Grand Father Clock or a high-end watch or Big Ben in London. You close your eyes and visualize this object. Now, once you have visualized that object give that object a name that makes sense for that object.

What you have accomplished here is setting a theme for your name. More importantly most people who will hear this name will think of the object. So let's call it Big Benny. In that name most people will think of Big Ben. They will think of the big clock in London which has an association with time. Your product is time management. Obviously this is a stretch. The point is these associations and getting people to instantly make those "visual" associations are what you are aiming for!

You can go out and test this familiarity with people with simple word games. You can say to your partner or friend what do you think of when I say "Time".

You can get a bunch of these answers and try to find one that creates a visual picture in the mind of the customer.

This is your path to a brand.

It may not be the best for SEO (Search Engine Optimization and domains), but like I have stated earlier in this book, who knows if domains and SEO are as important at brands and ultimately content. Trust me content and brands are king!

Write down all the potential objects or things that are related to you start-up. For instance, if you are making a car related app, write down car, auto, etc.

_____
_____
_____
_____

Visualize one of these objects in your mind. Write down a bunch of funny and cute names that make sense for the name of this object. Girl names, boy names, dog names make sense. If it was a car, then Love Bug may make sense.

_____
_____
_____
_____

Take some time to look around your room or space right now. For each object, think of something else that is familiar. Try to come up with a list of connected related familiar things to your start-up.

_____
_____
_____
_____

The most attractive thing you can ever say to An Angel investor is "I am not looking for Capital."

DAN GUDEMA

Personality

One of the things I love to see in names is personality. Personality is what gives your name it's special flavor. It tends to show off a theme and that you are different than the run of the mill competitor. And more importantly, if there is some part of a name that has some special flare to it, always take advantage of it. For instance if your name ends in "ride" then there should be some kind of vehicle or wheel or something to do with riding in the logo. I am not talking a real ride, but the personality of a ride. A ride could be a car, a motorcycle, a bicycle or a rocket ship. If it were CommerceRide, I would say "Ok, I get it, it has something to do with Commerce". That part is important. At least I would know that the personality is ride oriented. Later on the ride theme should be used as part of the logo as well.

As you think of a name for your business, what kind of personality are you trying to show the public?

The personality you choose will help you come up with a name. If you don't have a name yet, then thinking of this in advance will help you not just visualize the name, but you will be one step closer to arriving at the overall brand and the logo.

What Personality Do You Want Your Name To Portray?

A personality or persona is another word for a theme when it comes to names. For instance, Amazon.com has a jungle personality. Lyft is almost a robotic personality. Yahoo has always had a Swiss mountain climber personality with a yodeler.

To have personality in your name, you need to attach a tangible theme to your name. Some examples of themes are nature, winter, cars, animals like bears, spicy, fun, happy, professional, financial, dark, gamey, light, trees, sports, jovial, ancient, modern, mid-century modern or anything you can think of. You need to write a few words that automatically come to your mind when thinking of the business or product you are naming.

Your name should have a personality!

Some business names may not need personality. But businesses with personality are definitely memorable.

The personality tells the customer something about your flare and flavor. If you are funny sounding then you are probably a fun themed business. If you have a serious sounding name you should be a serious business. What would be a good name for a security firm? What kind of theme would be good for them? It's a guess but maybe a rocky mountain theme or a castle theme. These are impenetrable themes.

You need to apply the personality that fits with your business category or your business. This is how you start the process of knowing what personality and ultimately what name is right for your business. Once you do this, it is possible to come up with a list of potential names that fit this category and personality. You will be one step closer to determining an exceptional name.

I always look at names like Godaddy and Yahoo and they have a certain personality that is irreverent.

Is that what your business needs to stand-out from the pack?

Maybe.

It depends on what you are trying to accomplish.

You need to make a decision to stand-out and if that is right for you, go for it!

Is your strategy to stand-out and be immediately recognizable?

I have not heard of too many companies that do not want to stand out from the pack. You just have to make sure that your brand name stands out for the right reasons.

Is your name going to stand out in an appropriate way or an inappropriate way?

Once you make a choice about your personality you may not be able to easily change it. So choose this carefully.

What kind of personality do you want to explore for your name? An example would be something like speed or outdoors or natural or cutting edge. It could be most anything.

_____
_____
_____
_____

Think of words, not your name, that are in the theme you choose. If your theme is Universe, think of words like Stellar, Planet, Orbit, Galaxy, etc.

_____
_____
_____
_____

Take these theme words and combined them with industry words. If you came up with universe, and you are a hosting company, you could try writing down GalaxyHosting, HostingUniverse, PlanetHosting, etc. Many of these are real businesses. That's ok.

_____
_____
_____

Life is Short, Get A Name That Will Have An Impact And Will Never Be Forgotten

Humor

A doctor, priest and lawyer wanted to come up with a name for their tech start-up game of chance. The doctor wanted to call it The Game of Life. The priest wanted to call it The Game of Faith. The lawyer refused to answer. Why? He wanted to make sure all the contracts were signed. It is a bad joke. I am very bad at jokes.

So why can humor be so important in a name? Humor is a great way to remember a name! Whenever I reveal the name "Oops I'm Single" to somebody new, the reaction universally has been laughter. Why? Obviously it sounds funny. Most important is the laugher always, universally, happens when they hear or see the name. There is something about laughter that makes our cheeks rise and potentially our temperature change slightly. Your body changes physically. Maybe only slightly, but the change is enough to impact our brain. Laughter is almost universally involuntary. We don't go around faking laughter. It is the universal way of knowing what is and is not funny and gives us joy.

Physical To Emotional Self Being

When humor causes a physical reaction, that translates in our heads to an emotional reaction. Therefore my conclusion is that humor has an impact on your brain and your feelings about a name.

If your name can be funny or evoke a similar level of emotion, you are going to succeed in accomplishing all the other things this book talks about.

You will have accomplished memorability.

You will have accomplished familiarity.

You will have a brand name that can be easily differentiated and likeable.

I have run into a bunch of these names over the years. One of my favorites are double entendre names like "A Foreign Affair", setting up men with foreign woman. I helped a good friend decide on his name for his event technology business. He ended choosing the name Shmoozfest. It was funny and evoked emotion.

Choose A Name Humans Enjoy!

Names like this don't always make sense. They do, however, differentiate your name and business. Imagine you were looking at using either Cvent or Shmoozfest for a party. Hmm! Wonder which one is going to be more creative, funnier and a pleasure to work with.

Short, curt brand names are great and dominant right now in the market place, but the GoDaddy's of the future are going to be funnier, have more personality and be more human personality names. That ultimately leads to better branding.

Humor And The Edge

My cousin, the attempted comic, asked me recently what types of jokes are appropriate on stage and what is not appropriate?

You can ask yourself the same question and apply it to your tech start-up name. For on-stage comedy you know a joke is either offensive or does not work when the crowd does not laugh or boos. If the crowd laughs it is funny and appropriate. Even the least politically correct joke is funny and acceptable to the audience as long as there is no moment of silence! That's how you know a joke has failed. They don't get it or it is so insulting and over the line, it has been utterly rejected.

You can apply this to naming your tech start-up. Obviously you have gone too far if you use an inappropriate foul mouth word. You have gone too far if you using a stereo-type, ethnic group or inappropriate thing in the name.

You have to be your own audience.

You know when you are going to be insulting and you should have some intuition that your name could cause a problem!

You know there is a fine line for good and bad words and language.

Have kids? You know if your tech start-up name can't be said aloud in the house. That's when the name is probably inappropriate.

In the tech world we don't see a lot of funny names used too often. There are a few great ones like Yahoo! Yahoo! has always been a funny name. It is totally appropriate and memorable. You don't have to have a funny name, but if you can be funny, the benefits make it more attractive, approachable and easier to sell with.

What do you find funny about your business, industry or something related that is funny? It can be an incident or something that happened to your start-up which is funny.

_____
_____
_____
_____

Think of funny words that can be placed next to our in your tech start-up name. Things like Cool, Oops, Whatsup, hack, blink, joke, fun. Combine them.

_____
_____
_____
_____

Think of any fun variation to the name you have originally thought of for your business. For instance, Dominos was originally Dominics. Which sounds more fun?

_____
_____
_____
_____

Never use the words cash or money with investors. You are looking to raise capital!

Magnetism

Why are the Kardashians selling a billion dollars worth of TV and goods and services online?

The answer is they have a magnetic property about them. They are drawing in millions of viewers. They have created a storm of publicity and viewership unlike any other family in the reality city universe.

Things that are attractive stick to people. It just happens the Kardashians are physically attractive and emotionally attractive and that is why they get so much more attention. They allow you inside their wealthy lives and that allows for a certain amount of voyeurism that is real TV in the end.

How do we imbue your tech start-up name with attraction?

First off we need to figure out if that is something you desire. You need to make a decision. If you want to be attractive naturally, then look no further than names like Gilt and EyeCandy or Pop Candy.

If your tech start-up is in the realm of fashion or

lifestyle, even if it is a technical product, you need to consider the attraction level.

If you are selling an image technology used by these sophisticated industries you need to also consider your name being like-minded.

If you have a product that helps with photographing clothes for high end ecommerce, being called "Clothing Tech" may say what you do, but it is not sexy. Sexy sells.

If your tech product name was "Satin". That's sexy. These individual elements are sexy stuff and attractive.

A name does not have to convey the exact thing it does. It just have to produce in the customer's head a visual clue to what you do.

Names of recently successful start-ups like Uber and Lyft are somewhat attractive, but they are somewhat hollow. They are very memorable though and that is my number one criteria in choosing a name. We don't always feel the attraction to these simplistic names, but obviously they have created this attraction somehow!

Now, wouldn't it be nice to have an attractive name before your business even started. You can do this by going about making your name a little bit more sexy or attractive. This is especially required if you are selling to higher end clients.

So, how do you know if your name you have chosen is attractive? There are certain words that are attractive in our brains and ones that are not. It is an intuitive thing. You look at gold and platinum. Those words are attractive. You look at the words silver and copper. They are just not that attractive as gold and platinum. So we know a name is attractive in comparison to another name.

Things that are attractive have physical, emotional or psychological attraction built in. This means having a physical thing that is attractive in your name always helps. To have Ferrari in your name sounds over the top. But if that is really your name, then use it, like Trump. Having words which describe attractive things are also good for attraction.

Sometimes names are just naturally attractive.

NAMES

What are attractive elements that are related to your name? An example would be if you are a software company and you want to be known, you could have the world Million in your name.

_____
_____
_____
_____
_____

Can you think of business names that are attractive?

_____
_____
_____
_____
_____

Can you think of not so attractive names that you can modify by adding a modifier to come up with a more attractive name?

_____
_____
_____
_____
_____

DAN GUDEMA

It is very Easy to publish a book today. Writing the content is the hard part.

Names Are Marketing

In the late 80s I read a mesmerizing story about the renaming of a dozen of well-known books and plays in the 1950s. One story is Joseph Heller was going to name his book Catch-11, but he found out that there was a new movie called Ocean's 11. So he decided to switch to Catch-22. What is interesting about this, is the lexicon of American language and literature would have been completely different if Heller had stuck with the original title.

There are dozens of cases of book and movies being renamed. That's because the better name sells the book and especially sells the movie. Sometimes the name is the selling point and with a stinker of a movie behind the name. A good example of this was the movie Snakes On A Plane. It was not a very good movie, but most of us will never forget the name! Snakes On A Plane was an immediate attention getter.

Names represent images in our psyche for the rest of their lives. You always think of great books you have read in the past. Sometimes we quote these books or movies in our every day conversation.

Can you think of a business name that would have that staying power?

Book Titles Are Marketing

So, during the writing of this book, I had to think carefully about the title.

What would I name this book?.

My wife and I looked around at other tech start-up books and noticed a pattern. Each industry has a pattern or trend to how they are being named. My first couple books had long detailed names, like "How To Give An Elevator Pitch For Tech Start-Ups" and "Thinking Like A Start-Up". We determined that these long winded names are not in vogue. It seems like the pattern of book names are getting shorter and terser. That's when we decided to shorten this book to "Names". It was not a random decision. This will help it sell better. That is a marketing trend we followed!

For every industry and every market you need to look at the trend. Though you need to identify the trend, I also think you have an opportunity to find your own name individuality that breaks the trend. Maybe breaking the trend will get you noticed! Once again look at Godaddy. They are a hosting company. Most every other hosting company has a boring name. Ultimately you need to make sure that your name can succeed and be unique at the same time. Most people opt for something more conservative, but often the risk-takers are the big winners.

As you choose your domain name you will be making the a critical online marketing decision for your start-up. I recently worked with a start-up that used the name of their home town in their domain name and business name. That may have helped them get noticed in the beginning. Everybody will know they are local and accessible. Shortly afterwards the owner of the business complained to me that his ability to market himself outside of the town was limited. Well, what did he expect? So, how to resolve this. You need to think once again about what you are ultimately trying to accomplish with the name. Calling your business Peoria Web Design has its limitations. Calling your business Galaxy Web Design is ok but you will always have to say "we are located in Peoria". But a general name like Galaxy Web Design not tied to a location says something that has personality and can be used technically everywhere in terms of location.

Do you want to eventually be everywhere?

You don't need to use this guideline for your business. You have to weigh the positives and negatives of having a local name. It depends on each situation. You just need to understand the impact of your name and what difficulties it will present in the future to marketing your product or service.

How are you planning on marketing your business or service locally? Are you using a name as a marketing tool?

_____
_____
_____
_____
_____

Is your business tied to a physical location? If you are tied to a physical location can putting in a location or town, city name in your business name help or hurt you long term?

_____
_____
_____
_____
_____

Can you come up with a name that adds marketing savvy to your name? Think about what sells and do you have those words in your name?

_____
_____
_____
_____

Good stories are about the moment when somebody's life changes.

Duba Leibell

Business Name vs. Product Name vs. Domain Name

As the Internet rolled into our lives in the 90s, there came about a shift in how names were meted out. Before the Internet and all these domain names, you would come up with just a business name. Under that business name was the product or service name, if you needed one.

Now we have the domain name to deal with.

This domain name business is a big business. For the first 15 years of the Internet it was everything. In fact for many years the domain name was the business and the product name. And you had to control that domain name to control the brand. This lead to a big conflict between the owner of the domain Nissan.com and Nissan Corp. Domain squatters generally have lost the battle with Trademark holders. Of course legally using a trademark in your domain name could result in a cease and desist letter telling you to hand over the domain. One of my clients told me he owned Gucci.com and other top brand domain names, but when the Internet grew in popularity, these brands came knocking on his door with their lawyers and he had to relent or have the domain taken by a court order.

With mobile apps, the domain name is not so important, because there is no domain name per se. You look up the name on Apple iTunes or Android Playstore. It looks like Trademark and brand is coming back in fashion because of mobile apps. And tons of mobile app makers are free from the constraint of the domain name. They can call their app whatever they want as long as that app name is not already used exactly and settle for a lesser domain extension like .io, .co, and 100 other extensions for their actual domain name. These domain name extensions may be ok for a mobile app. So, not everything is taken. You have to focus on your brand, not what .com names are available.

Names & Search Engine Optimization

On the other hand, being that I know a little bit about SEO, Search Engine Optimization, it is important to have a good .com domain in order to get listed properly by Google. As a tech person, if that is you, you may already know a lot about search engines, rich snippets and getting ranked in natural search.

Of course domain names are important! I may be contradicting myself here, because SEO is different than Branding. Great domains can make or break your business. However, the content you produce is just as important.

Some people choose a name based on the exact search terms people are putting in. This is a great way to get found. It goes against what I have been saying about branding, but depending on your business, that may not matter. It matters less by the day. If our speed dating venture had been named SpeedDatingUnited.com we would have run some events and gotten some traction. We may have been just a big. We would have been worse off in terms of being memorable. If we did not care at all about return traffic then SpeedDatingUnited.com would have worked.

Having a very generic name saying exactly what you do will get you traffic for new customers, however, without any unique way of remembering that name, return traffic would have suffered. Your easy to find domain name would have left your customers brains because it was not that memorable!

Having your keywords start your domain names is a strategy I do recommend if you are in a commodity-like business. An online commodity-like business means that people are searching generically for those words, not your brand. It means that there really is no difference between what you sell and the competition. If people are looking to buy gold, then being BuyGold.com makes sense then. The problem is the domain BuyGold.com is going to cost you because it is not available for a low price.

Mobile Sites Have No SEO

Just the domain name alone is not the only answer to getting a start-up off the ground. We have met with several start-ups which have built beautiful mobile apps that can't seem to get any traction. Why? It is quite simple. They need to have a web presence in order to get found and to get traction without spending money on advertising. Websites, web pages with text and HTML produces content that is indexed on Google.

Mobile apps don't generate content!

This is a hard lesson for mobile app entrepreneurs

to learn. It is a very important issue for mobile app start-ups to deal with because they can't get easily found on Google unless they build a traditional website. That is why we have recommended several startups building mobile apps to go back and build a real website that Google can index. Otherwise the only way they are getting traffic is ad campaigns, word of mouth and running media like TV, Radio and PPC campaigns. That is costly! They are missing out on the biggest source of free traffic known to man-kind. Even Pay Per Click spending for mobile app companies can be a bit of wasteful spending, because it just drives traffic to iTunes and Android Play Store, not your real web presence.

While mobile apps are still growing and a very important channel today, using words in actual websites helps you get found organically or without paying. So in this case your name and your content can be the most important thing you have to get noticed. Words are the reason why many tech ventures succeed or fail. But this is not always about the domain name. It is almost certainly is about the content.

When you look at a Reddit.com or a Craigslist.com, you see a lot of old style html content. It does not matter. Google loves their ever creating never ending content building. Did the names of these businesses really matter in the end? The answer is somewhere in between a yes and a no. These two sites could have easy been Readit.com and Bobslist.com. So, maybe website names are not everything now that content is king and brands are in vogue again.

Brands are what dominate the mobile app market. Just look at Angry Birds, Candy Crush and MindCraft. At least I learned something from my kids!

NAMES

Are you choosing a name for a website, a physical business or for a physical product? What are the different names you have chosen for the business, website and product or service?

_____
_____
_____
_____

What are the key words customers would put into Google to find your business?

_____
_____
_____
_____
_____

What alternative domain names may you want to consider for your business? If you can not acquire the name you want, can you find an alternative with the right key words in the name or a new kind of domain extension?

_____
_____
_____
_____

Hurrydate was 3 minutes, Pre-Dating was 6 minutes, 8MinuteDating was 8 minutes, but I needed 20 minutes. so I met nobody!

Dan Gudema
On trying to meet a woman Speed dating

DAN GUDEMA

Unconsciously Naming

For some of us, we actually can create our new tech start-up name in our dreams or unconsciously while we are not focusing on the problem. I've done it!

When you go to bed, you will notice that your brain continues working though you are sleeping. I have found myself waking up in the middle of the night thinking of solving a problem like coming up with a good name. You focus in on the problem and try to let your unconscious mind take over.

Unconscious thinking is a way of solving issues and letting your mind work on a problem, even while you sleep or go about your everyday activities. Some may say this leads to a bad night of sleep. I find no problems with it. Surprisingly, you may find in the morning your mind has suddenly come up with a name.

The biggest problem about working out a problem unconsciously while sleeping is if you come up with a great name or solution to a problem, you typically have to act immediately or you will forget the name. You have to write down what you thought of before you lose it. You would have to get up from your sleep to do this. You can solve more than just coming up with names this way. It is possible to come up with complete solutions while you sleep!

I had this happen to me about a year ago. I was working on a UI problem for our mobile app tech start-up called Krowde at the time. At that point in time we had a User Interface that was problematic and confusing. We knew that the UI problem needed to be solved. I was not specifically working on this particular problem directly. I was working on another issue at the time. (That is how it generally works. You are one working on one thing and the answer for the other thing just happens.) For some reason suddenly in the middle of the night I saw the layout of the Roku screen from Netflix. However, I saw it laid out in a way that would fit our needs for our start-up. I got up. I wrote down all the designs I was seeing in my head. The next day we changed the UI direction of the company.

Things happen in our minds at night when we can relax. It allows solutions to come us as opposed to us searching for a solution consciously. The same was true for Bill Gates and Microsoft. He was up all night playing with the early Internet. He never went to sleep. When he got up and went to work in the morning, he decided to change the entire direction of the business.

It is a bit Zen, but often the less you work on a big audacious tech problem or coming up with a name, the more likely you will find a solution.

Your mind continues to work on problems all the time, though you are not exactly aware of it.

And solutions often come to us in one moment.

I have been through a couple situations where my unconscious mind suddenly figured out a name, a problem or a design pattern. I also notice that when I do a lot of complex work, like object oriented programming or solving crossword puzzles or play complicated Japanese Sudoku that somehow my mind seems to get all tuned up.

At the end of one of these days is the point when I suddenly have answers come to me. So theoretically if this is true, you should prepare the question in your head at the beginning of the day.

What will be the name of this company?

What will be the name of this product?

And on that day you have set this question for yourself, you just go about doing your work. At the end of the day, you may suddenly have an answer. Weird how the brain works.

NAMES

Write down the question to what you want to accomplish today. Do you want to find a business name, a product or service name or a good domain name?

_____
_____
_____
_____
_____

Keep this book handy and write down any names that come to you over the next 24 hours?

_____
_____
_____
_____
_____

What other problems do you want to solve during this period? write down those problems here as well. When you return to this book, you have an answer.

_____
_____
_____
_____

She was a 718, I was a 212. I was going to become a 908 and she was moving on to 732.
Would we ever meet?

From a series of branding ads introducing new area codes in the New York Area (sic).

The Name Shortening Game

In the 1980s came a trend that continues to this date. Companies with long names started to shorten their names in an attempt to stay with current trends to make themselves more corporate and possibly serve a larger market. For instance being stuck in a certain market segment could forever limit a business and their growth so thought MBA Professors at the time.

And suddenly long corporate brand names were being changed as part of the trend. Some did it to avoid a word or service that they wanted to not be associated with. Some did it because others did it. It was all theoretical. Kentucky Fried Chicken became KFC. Radio Shack became The Shack. Pizza Hut became known as The Hut. Then there was QVC and HSN. Even recently Plenty of Fish started to be known as POF. Many corporate brands went online with these initials as a shorter way to be found. The initials worked to some extent.

Another theory is they all want to become the next ABC, CBS or NBC. Those media companies could evolve and grow into any business they choose without explaining to customers why!

The biggest Internet player with this fad was America Online. They became AOL. That was supposed to help them be more expansive globally in what they did. They could say they are not just a dial up company but a media company, a news company, a search engine. A lot of things. Maybe it was meant to help them grow outside the US. Either way it really did not help in the end. If you remember they ended up in a mega merger with Time Warner. It did help tremendously with users remembering the URL to get to their site.

Apparently some of the shortened names lead to quicker and better discovery on search engines, less characters and direct access to their sites. So for this reason it made some technical sense. They saved 10 characters a day times 30 million visitors... Do the byte math.

The big question today is does it make sense to choose a 3 letter domain today like this and brand yourself this way.

Think about it.

You decide to name your business POP.com. That sounds great to a domainer. Domainers are domain owners who horde large numbers of domains for resale. Problem is that the very short name like this is not very brand-able or memorable. They tend to fall into the types of name that require even more spending to convince people they are a brand. This is just my opinion... Brand is everything to me and very short names are just don't stick as easily in my head as memorable words (unless they spend a lot of money on advertising to make you remember!).

"When developing a great brand it is important to think about your website address and make sure a good domain name is available .dot com is preferred. And if your preferred domain isn't available check to see if you can buy it - often the owner will sell for a reasonable price. Lastly, check pto.gov for trademark availability - many people pick a brand, get the domain only to get blocked by a trademark"

Jay Berkowitz, Ten Golden Rules

Name Examples

By looking over these names, we are going to analyze why these names were used by recent start-ups, why they work well and why some don't work well. Remember the ones that don't make too much sense or are not very strong often needed vast ad budgets to make the public believe they are the name or brand they have become.

Some of these names are very recognizable. Some we love for their simplicity. Some we remember because they were just so disruptive sounding that we will never forget them.

I have reached back into the ghosts of Internet past, present and future with these names. What I have done is taken the criteria of memorability, familiarity, personality and does it say what it does and applied each of these theories to each name. Here are some notes and why I think they worked or did not work well. This is all my opinion.

I tried approaching these names as though I was working for you and had to help you make a decision on the name of your startup company! By reading through all these names and notes you will start to see a pattern to why names work and why they don't. Where some of these names had weaknesses in the name, they often made up for it with a great service. So you can make a bad name work. I've done it.

Search Engines:

Yahoo Memorable, Reminds us of a Yodeler, Seems to attract me, but says nothing about what it does!

Google Memorable, Reminds me of a math problem, Seems to attract me, but once again it originally said very little about what it does!

AltaVista It was not so memorable, It was familiar of a mountain range, There was something attractive about Vista, which has something to do with skylines, Today you would not be able to guess what it did back then.

Bing Pretty memorable, Very familiar sounding, I don't find this name attractive at all, Says nothing about what it does.

DogPile Not memorable, completely familiar, but not for a good reason since you know what it reminds me of, Completely unattractive name, says nothing to me about what it does! Need I say more about why it did not succeed.

AOL Very Memorable, I don't find it very familiar with anything become it was initials, Not an attractive name, says nothing about what it does, though America Online did!

Ecommerce:

eBay I find it very memorable, Very familiar with the word Bay or body of water, I think it is an attractive name, but says nothing about what it does!

Amazon Extremely memorable, Very familiar because of Amazon River image, Average attraction and nothing funny about that name though it has some personality, says nothing about what it does!

BestBuy Not that memorable, Extremely Familiar sounding. Ok attraction-wise, because Best is a good word, Says what it does!

Gilt Very Memorable, somewhat familiar, Extremely attractive, says nothing about what it does!

Woot Very Memorable, a bit familiar in that it reminds me of a sound, not so attractive to me, says nothing about what it does!

Share Economy:

Lyft Pretty memorable, Extremely familiar, Not so attractive to me, says everything about what it does!

Uber Pretty memorable, Not familiar of anything, Seems to attract me, and says nothing about what it does!

AirBNB Memorable, Very familiar sounding name, Not so attractive name to me, says enough about what it does!

AngiesList Very memorable, Familiar sounding, Not too attractive name to me, not too close to what it does!

Social Networks:

Facebook Memorable, Very familiar sounding name, Not so attractive name to me, says what it does! Zuckerberg made it work, even though it was not the best name ever! So names don't have to be perfect.

Twitter Very Memorable, Very familiar sounding name, Not so attractive name to me, and it really does not say what it does. In fact I know many people who still don't get it! However, this is a case where the name created a verb, TO TWEET. That was a big accomplishment.

Linkedin Very Memorable, Somewhat familiar name, Average attractiveness, says enough about what it does!

Pinterest Not so memorable, a familiar

sounding name, Not so attractive name to me, says nothing about what it does!

Path Not memorable, Very familiar sounding name, Not so attractive name to me, have no idea what it does!

WhatsApp Extremely Memorable, Somewhat familiar name, Not too attractive, says exactly what it does!

Snapchat Somewhat Memorable, Extremely familiar name, Not attractive at all to me, says what it does!

Geocities Not Memorable, Familiar sounding name, Not attractive at all to me, though it kind of said what it did!

Tripod Not Memorable, Not too familiar name, Not attractive at all to me, did not say what it does and believe it or not it is still around!

Job Sites:

Monster Extremely Memorable, Very familiar name, Not very attractive or shiny, Says nothing about what it does.

Hotjobs Memorable, Very familiar sounding name, Not so attractive name to me, says enough about what it does!

Careerbuilder Not very memorable, Very familiar name because it has career in it, Not so attractive name to me, says enough about what it does!

Dating:

Match Not that memorable a name, Very familiar sounding name which could mean a lot of things, I don't find it very attractive, It says what it does but not specific to an industry.

eHarmony Extremely Memorable, Very familiar name, Very Attractive, does not say what it does!

Plenty Of Fish Very Memorable, Extremely familiar sounding name, Not so attractive name to me, does not says enough about what it does!

Red Hot Pie Very Memorable, Very familiar name, Not attractive at all, does not say anything about what it does (for Americans)!

Tinder Somewhat Memorable, Very familiar sounding name, Not the most attractive name to me, says very little about what it does!

Grinder Memorable, Very familiar sounding name, Not attractive name at all and very ugly sounding, says just a little bit about what it does!

Skout Not too Memorable, Very familiar sounding name, Not too attractive name to me, says what it does well!

Pets

Pets.com Extremely memorable, Extremely familiar sounding name, Average attractive name to me, says what it does!

PetSmart Very Memorable, Very familiar sounding name, Pretty attractive to me, says what it does a bit!

Browsers:

Explorer Not memorable, Very familiar sounding name, Not too attractive name to me, Says what it does.

Firefox Very memorable, Very familiar sounding name, Pretty attractive name, Says nothing about what it does!

Chrome Not too Memorable, Very familiar sounding name, Very attractive name, Does not say what it does!

Email Providers:

Hotmail Very memorable, Very familiar sounding name, Very attractive name to me, Says what it does.

Gmail Not too memorable, Familiar sounding name with the word mail in it, Not an attractive name, Says something about what it does!

Inbox.com Not memorable, Familiar sounding name, Not attractive name, Does say what it does!

NAMES

The Masses Are Asses!

Alexander Hamilton

DAN GUDEMA

How To Not Name Your Company

I am very much against naming decisions by consensus. They are quite often failures at finding a name. One of the most common exercises I have seen companies come up with is the old time voting method. It seems like a rational idea. You ask everybody in the company to think of a name. You get all those names to compare and contrast against each other in a big list. You then ask all the employees or friends of the founder to pick one or rank them by what they find to be the best name. It is a voting process and you end up with a winner. Problem is that the winner could actually be everybody's second choice. Also, the winner will probably be mediocre.

Look at Godaddy. If the founder of Godaddy had asked his employees to vote on a company name, they would have ended up Domains.com. Hope you get my point on this. Consensus naming results in less risky, less personality driven name results!

This is just my irrational opinion, but I have only

seen this scientific method approach fail. It fails to come up with a name that is amazing. You want to be extraordinary!

Being extraordinary is what will make your company successful.

Even worse, you end up choosing a name that the mob of people wants. Not that you know better than the mob, but sometimes you do. If these are employees they don't want to take a risk. This is like a virus. It invades their minds. They don't make a mistake by choosing the mediocre name! If it is your business or baby, you need to hatch that name and make a command decision!

Company Leaderless-ness

The lack of leadership or command decision making in big corporate entities is an amazingly bad thing. One of the reasons there are 3 branches of US government are so some people can make decisions without being influenced, like the Supreme Court. Sometimes select people with more information do know better than the masses who only have a limited view of things. John Adams stated "The Masses Are Asses".

Democracy is great, but not for the name of your business. If you are in charge, make a decision. Come up with your reasons, but obviously stick to your guns and drive that name forward.

There are a ton of average names that have proven they are average. A good example of this is CareerBuilder.com. Years ago I heard the man who ran this division of Knight-Ridder say that no matter how much money they spent on advertising, every time they surveyed people about which job site they could remember off the top of their heads, the public still would come up first with Monster and second with Hotjobs.com. How they ended up with CareerBuilder.com is simple. A group of employees or executives at that company came up with that name, an average name, so they would not be blamed for their mistake. It's a simple problem that happens a lot. Imagine a group of people working together on a unique oil painting at the same time. The end result is a mishmash that makes nobody happy.

Other Big Mistakes To Avoid

Obviously using foul language or ethnic slurs or something insulting in the name will be a problem. We are better than that. You need to be proud of your name. If you have to hide it from people that is not good!

I experienced one specific problem working with a start-up company that has a misspelling in the name that they had decided on using. This is not the same thing as purposeful branded misspelling. I have created a bunch of names where I switched the C with a K. Lyft for instance is fine. They switched the I for a Y. That makes some sense in my mind. It is a variation of the spelling, not an outright spelling error. It is brand that is purposeful. I have added an extra E to a name to give it a different brand feel. All of these variations are fine and purposeful. If your name probably should be Pot Pie Bakery and you make your name Pot Pie Backery, that is just wrong. Pot Pi Bakery could actually work though. It has a double entendre with a math theme. If you are supposed be "Compression Fittings" and because that domain name was not available you decided to name the company "Compresion Fittings", that is a very bad decision!

Then there is another problem that has occurred, especially with domain names where the name has one meaning, but if you read it differently it has a bad meaning, like "Computers Exchange". You get the domain name ComputersExchange.com.

NAMES

However, if you read it this way, ComputerSexChange.com, you may have a problem. This is a minor little hiccup that can occur. Just make sure there is no secondary name hidden in the domain name.

We have put together a list of poorly chosen names below. Some are bad just because they are bad and others are bad because they have in them another hidden name the founders missed.

Some Of The Worst Online Web Startup Names Ever Chosen:

Fashism Did this fashion site realize that sounding like a foreign dictatorship would not be attractive?

Lawdingo Not a great thing to be in the legal field and have the name of a wild dog in your name!

Xobni Creative because it was inbox spelled backwards, but who would get that!

Fairtilizer Not sure what these guys did, but let's just say that having something that reminds of us manure is not good.

US Likey There's a difference between being cute and being stupid!

Twisper This was a case of trying to be between Twitter and Whisper, but overall nobody got it!

Name Examples Where They Ended Up With A Negative Hidden Meaning:

ITScrap — ItsCrap
PenIsland — PenisLand
WhoRepresents — WhorePresents
ExpertsExchange — ExpertSexChange
NOBjs.org — NoBJs.org
MasterBaitonLine — MasterBaitOnline
TherapistInABox — TheRapistInABox
TherapistFinder.com — TheRapistFinder
Dicksonweb.com — DicksOnWeb
KidsExchange.net — KidSexChange
TeachersTalking.org — TeacherStalking
MoleStationNursery — MolestationNursery

NAMES

NAMES

Names should not make you confused. They should either make you laugh or make you never forget them.

A Few Final Words

This book is my third book for Tech Startups. The intent of this book is to help tech start-ups come up with great names for their start-ups. A great technology company or product with a hard to understand or ill conceived name can be a major problem when selling to customers. If you need to find a new name or rename your tech start-up then that's what this book is about. The first book I wrote was called *Thinking Like A Start-Up*. It was meant for both start-ups and large corporate staff to read. We should all think like a start-up. You can find it on Amazon.com in print or in a Kindle version. That book was based on my blog entries from 2009 to 2014. That book gave me the inspiration to write my second book *How To Give An Elevator Pitch For Start-Ups* and then this book *Names*. To help start-ups figure out a good name, I did not want to sell a 400 page book, because most tech start-ups need a short book and not a complete guide to everything. If you need to find a name for your company or product, you need to find your name today. So, if you need to find a name today, by this book today! This book was created by **StartupPOP** and is the second in a series I am calling **Tools For Tech Start-Ups**. Please buy each one as you need them. Good Luck!

Thanks To These Startups

I also wanted to thank all the startups who presented at The Greenhouse in 2014 and 2015 who participated in our Start-Up Tech Pitch Events:

adFroogle, Aerobyte, ActivePark, Apparition Mobile, Apretaste, Avila Stores, Aqua TV, ArrestSOS, beTen, BCD Software, BYL Network, caddyDRONE, Counsel On The Go, DL Alert Pro, eCalypse, EvictionsPro, Everyware, Frelp, Friendly Reminders, GameMerce, Game Masters Solutions, Glince, Global Boat Works, GPS for Piano, HeadyFoods, Greet, Gyfu, Hello Show, iLumenfi, Jinglz, Kanyu, Liquidbricks, LunchMoney, Mission Tuition, MobiDox, Mrecruit, Neuromore, Pickk, Previte, Prom.ly, Prototype, Puppy Play Dates, House, Referrizer, Roizo, Sierra Lifestyle, Inc., Seyopa, SKY H2O, Smitz Laboratories Corp, SociallyBuzz, Stand4, Sygnol Analytics, Take Up Code, TapNSell, TGL Film, The Animal Social Network, Tinker University, TightTalk Electronics, ToneLive, TruVisibility, Tudor Ice Company, uRemix, UseMyBenefits.com, Vivarena, Young Makers Lab, Well Done Wood, Who Ya Got, Wiki Beach Real Estate, Zeekah

Quoted People

Who is Martin Lindstrom? Martin Linstrom has written the book Buyology and coined the term Smash Your Brand and uses brain scans to analyze the impact of marketing on the human brain.

Who Is John Kemp? John, a good friend of mine has the distinction of being the rare Scottish African American as he puts it. John founded both CompuStaff and Skillsoft, multi-million dollar IT job firms and more recently eCannex.

Who is Jay Berkowitz? Jay is a successful online marketer and speaker based in South Florida best known for his book entitled "10 Golden Rules". Jay has been quoted and published in most business journals and newspapers in South Florida.

Who is Duba Leibell? Duba is an active screenwriter and writing professor at the University of Miami in South Florida. Her specialty, outside of a spec script, like Miss Havana, has been story development.

Alexander Hamilton was one of the founders of United States and the US financial system.

Your Reading List

Throughout my books I mention some of my favorite start-up books. This is your reading list. If you are a tech start-up and have not read these books, you need to start now!

Get Real: The Smarter, Faster, Easier Way to Build a Successful Web Application by Jason Fried, David Heinemeier Hansson and Matthew Linderman
Rework by Jason Fried, David Heinemeier Hansson
The Art of The Start by Guy Kawasaki
Reality Check by Guy Kawasaki
Rules For Revolutionaries by Guy Kawasaki
Don't Make Me Think by Steve Krug
Do More, Faster by Brad Feld
World Famous by David Tyreman
The Wisdom Of Crowds by James Surowiecki
What the Dog Saw by Malcom Gladwell
Outliers by Malcom Gladwell
The Launch Pad by Randall Stross
The Lean Startup by Eric Ries
All Marketers Are Liars by Seth Godin
Wikinomics by Don Tapscott and Anthony D. Williams
Getting Into Your Customer's Head by Kevin Davis
SLIDE:OLOGY by Diane Duarte
Resonate by Diane Duarte
You Got To Believed To Be Heard by Bert Decker
Inevitable Surprises by Peter Schwartz
Authority by Nathan Barry

About The Author

Though Dan Gudema aspired to be a writer as a kid, he was never able to fulfill that journey up till recently. Dan has worked as a corporate manager, programmer, entrepreneur and consultant. Dan is a fixture in the Start-Up community in South Florida. Dan has worked as an IT and Web manager or consultant for Bell Atlantic Mobile, abc Distributing, NTT Corporation/Verio Inc., Office Depot and The Limited. In 2001 Dan co-founded and developed as a programmer Pre-Dating Speed Dating, which became the largest speed dating company in the US. It was sold to Cupid.com in 2004. Dan is the founder of StartupPOP, a Tech Startup Pitch Event which began in Boca Raton, FL. Please go to StartupPOP.com and get on his mailing list. Dan is also a Tech Startup Consultant working with a variety of local tech startups! Originally from Parsippany, NJ, Dan moved to South Florida in 1997. Dan attended the University of Maryland for his BA and has an MBA from Florida Atlantic University. In 2004, Dan won a business plan contest at FAU while in their MBA program. Please visit Amazon.com for more books by Dan Gudema or email Dan with your thoughts at dan@startuppop.com or connect on twitter @dgudema or Linkedin!

www.ingramcontent.com/pod-product-compliance
Lightning Source LLC
Chambersburg PA
CBHW051808170526
45167CB00005B/1932